BRITISH RAIL
TRACTION
MAINTENANCE DEPOTS
1974–1993

Part 3: Wales & Scotland

MICHAEL RHODES

Published by Platform 5 Publishing Ltd,
52 Broadfield Road, Sheffield, S8 0XJ. England.

Printed in England by The Amadeus Press, Cleckheaton, West Yorkshire.

ISBN: 978 1 915984 15 9

© 2023 Platform 5 Publishing Ltd. Copyright in the photographs remains with Michael Rhodes. All rights reserved. No part of this publication may be reproduced or transmitted in any form or by any means electronic, mechanical, photocopying, recording or otherwise, without prior permission of the publisher.

Above: This general view of Severn Tunnel Junction gives an idea of vast numbers of locomotives that could be found stabled at depots during the 1970s and 1980s, especially during weekends when lower volumes of freight were moved by rail. On Saturday 23 January 1982, there were at least 25 locomotives stabled at Severn Tunnel Junction, with a variety of representatives from Classes 08, 25, 31, 37, 45 and 47. From left to right, the engines at the front of the four rows are 47247, 31152, 45106 and 08901.

Front cover: On 23 July 1983 all was quiet at Margam depot in South Wales, which gave me the opportunity to clamber up a lighting mast and capture this view from the south end of the site. From left to right, the locomotives that are visible at the end of each row are 47066, 45064, 37247, 47246, 08361 and 47087.

Back cover: Haymarket depot is located two miles west of Edinburgh Waverley station and is easily visible from passing trains. An impressive total of 39 locomotives was to be found there on 9 July 1978, with representatives from Classes 08, 20, 25, 26, 27, 40, 46, 47 and 55 (a complete list of these can be found on page 62). Some of the traction was captured in this photograph, with 27210 prominent in the centre and 25087 to its right. Another 27 and a 47 are stabled behind and the end of a Class 40 can be seen inside the shed.

Previous page: Polmadie depot is located just south of Glasgow city centre and remains in use today. If we rewind by more than 45 years, to 14 August 1978, this selection of locomotives was found in these recently-laid sidings, which are on the far side of the West Coast Main Line to the main depot facilities. From left to right are 25246 and 27034 on the first siding, followed by 20117, 20108, 20126 & 20093. To their right 26026, then 37155 and finally 08853, 08733, 08421, 08719, 40014 and 27020 on the right. In addition, out of view were 08719, 20020, 20049, 20095, 20105, 20107, 25287 and 25288.

CONTENTS

Introduction 4

Wales 5

    Holyhead 5

    Llandudno Junction 7

    Cardiff Canton 8

    Margam 23

    Landore 26

    Ebbw Junction 34

    Severn Tunnel Junction 39

Scotland 44

    Inverness 44

    Aberdeen Ferryhill 51

    Dundee 53

    Dunfermline Townhill 54

    Grangemouth 59

    Haymarket 62

    Eastfield 70

    Glasgow Works 75

    Polmadie 77

    Hamilton 82

    Motherwell 84

    Ayr 92

TRACTION MAINTENANCE DEPOTS

INTRODUCTION

Welcome to this third and final volume which presents a selection of my photographs of British traction maintenance depots. The predominant function of the depots in South Wales and Central Scotland was to service the freight motive power that worked to and from the surrounding coalfields and steelworks. In contrast, the traffic in North Wales and Northern Scotland was almost exclusively passenger and so the allocations of the depots in these regions tended to reflect this. South Wales had two major depots, Cardiff Canton and Swansea Landore. Canton was the biggest depot in Wales and often held more than 50 locomotives during a weekend, whilst Landore wasn't as large and many locomotives would be stabled in the nearby Swansea Docks rather than on the main depot. Similarly, in Scotland there were two major depots at Edinburgh Haymarket and Glasgow Eastfield, both of which could amass 50 locomotives on a good weekend. Of course things have changed radically since the decades covered by this series. For example, the largest locomotive depot in Scotland, Eastfield, was closed and demolished over 20 years ago and a smaller diesel multiple unit facility now stands on the site. Likewise, the iconic footbridge at Wales' largest depot, Cardiff Canton, was demolished in 2014 and the trains now seen passing through Cardiff and Canton are very different to those illustrated in this book.

Other changes that have radically altered the depots in both Wales and Scotland are the move away from locomotive hauled passenger trains and the almost complete disappearance of the coal mining and steelmaking industries. Very few coal trains now run and the steelmaking plants at Ravenscraig and Llanwern have closed. Consequently, dozens of freight-only routes have been closed and lifted, or have been mothballed.

The reader might well ask why the period from 1974 to 1993 has been chosen. Its start was dictated by the time that I began photographing depots and its end was determined by several factors. Concerns about trespassing were becoming greater as we entered the 1990s. At the same time I was no longer a student or junior doctor, but was working as a lecturer in surgery in Cardiff from 1992 and I was concerned that getting arrested for visiting an engine shed would be irresponsible. Palisade fencing was also appearing around depots and I can remember finding that entry into sites such as Canton and Immingham was suddenly impossible due to the new fencing. The tradition of "shed bashing" was accepted as normal in the 1960s, tolerated in the 1970s and had turned into trespass with consequences by the early 1990s.

This series is not a text book or historical summary of all the depots, but rather a recollection of hundreds of hours of a misspent youth. Some major depots hardly feature because I made few visits to them or didn't take any photographs there. On the other hand, my "home" depots, Cardiff Canton and Severn Tunnel Junction are perhaps over represented because I lived near to these. Hopefully this selection of images will bring back many happy memories for those of us who enjoyed the freedoms of trainspotting in the 1970s and 1980s.

Michael Rhodes
Thurston, 2023

Above: On 13 September 1979, during a thorough exploration of Inverness depot, 26046 was one of the many locos found stabled there. It is seen beside the refueling point on the north side of the depot.

WALES

HOLYHEAD

Beginning with the most north-westerly facility in Wales, the depot at Holyhead was a five-minute walk from the station. It consisted of the former four-road steam shed, which other than the addition of a refuelling canopy to the east, had received very few modifications. The depot lost its allocation in 1986 and was demolished in 1989. There was a notable stabling point on the nearby Holyhead Breakwater, which was unusual in that it was no longer connected to the rest of the railway network.

Above: On 5 August 1976, 40179 and 08025 were to be found on shed. Also present on the depot that day were 40042 and 40119.

TRACTION MAINTENANCE DEPOTS

Above: On the same day in 1976, 01001 was hiding away inside the breakwater shed and sadly my image of it was very blurred. Classmate 01002 was to be found outside on the breakwater.

Above: Two years later, on 1 August 1978, 40030 was found inside the old steam depot at Holyhead. 40030 entered service as early as 1959 and went on to be withdrawn in 1983, before being scrapped at Crewe Works in 1984. The former steam depot building lasted a little bit longer; it was demolished in 1989 to make way for a smaller two-track facility which remains in place today.

Right: Also on 1 August 1978, 40013 and 25166 were stabled at Holyhead's fuelling point, as seen from the shelter of the steam shed while the heavens opened.

LLANDUDNO JUNCTION

In the Locoshed Directory, Llandudno Junction was described as being just across the tracks from the station's platform and accessible by a 15-minute walk from Llandudno Junction station. In the directory's final edition it was suggested that one might find a single locomotive stabled there during weekends and none during the week, which was my experience. After the depot was demolished at the turn of the century, a new road was built over the railway, immediately west of Llandudno Junction station. This travelled over the site of the former depot and in recognition of this, the road was given the highly unusual name of "Ffordd 6G Road" which is believed to be the only road name that contains a BR depot code, 6G being that of the former facility at Llandudno Junction.

Above: By the summer of 1976, when this image was taken, Llandudno Junction depot was on its last legs, as it was usually only used on summer Saturdays when holiday traffic to Llandudno and the rest of North Wales was heavy. On 5 August 1976, 40030 was found stabled there, bringing added interest among the stored carriages that were present.

TRACTION MAINTENANCE DEPOTS

CARDIFF CANTON

The new diesel depot at Canton was built on the site of the former steam depot and opened in 1964. The refuelling shed was refashioned from one of the steam depot buildings, whilst the vast heavy maintenance shed was a new build. There was also an eight-road carriage shed for the large DMU fleet based in Cardiff. Because the passenger services for London nearly always started from Swansea, the motive power for these was based at Landore. Most of the locomotives allocated to Canton were for freight traffic and this is reflected in what was found both there and at the stabling points linked to the depot. These were at Radyr Yard, Barry, Aberdare, Cardiff East Dock and Windsor Road Goods Depot. As the mines in South Wales closed one by one and steel production reduced to just the one steel making plant in Port Talbot and one tinplate factory in Trostre, the raison d'etre for Cardiff Canton vanished. It closed as a maintenance facility in 2004 and the famous footbridge from De Crouche Place was dismantled in 2014.

On a personal note, one fateful day in 1972, Cardiff Canton, or more specifically the footbridge over the South Wales Main Line (SWML), is where it all began for me! I had always been interested in railways and had built a model railway, but couldn't see the point of "train spotting". That was until a school friend persuaded me to visit Canton's sheds and I was then hooked. As evidenced by the images in this section, Canton was a remarkably easy depot to wander round. The standard circuit was over the footbridge and alongside the northern edge of the refuelling shed, round the back of the complex and across to the large maintenance depot. This was entered at the rear and exited at the front, adjacent to the main yard office, which had to be walked past to get back to the footbridge, safe in the knowledge that all the numbers on the depot had already been recorded. Often on Saturdays and Sundays there were several dozen spotters on the footbridge or in various nooks and crannies around the depot, so popular was Canton.

Right: Christmas Day in 1978 saw Canton depot packed. My notebook records that I obtained permission from the lone watchman, a Mr James from Merthyr Tydfil, who allowed me to climb the lighting mast on the condition that I sent him a print of my photograph! The locomotives that were on shed that day are listed in Table 1.

Below right: Class 52 1013 "WESTERN RANGER" stands next to 31293 on 5 February 1977, just three weeks before the end for the Westerns. It was stabled at Canton as a backup loco for D1023 which was used to haul a Western special from Cardiff to London Paddington and back that day. Another 31 is visible behind 1013 and a gaggle of spotters can be seen on the well-used footbridge that provided access to Canton depot.

Table 1: The locos present at Cardiff Canton on two dates in the 1970s. In addition, on 5 February 1974, a total of 72 DMU vehicles were recorded.

Class	Locos on 5 February 1974	Locos on 25 December 1978
03	None	03144
08	3258, 3266, 3419, 3424, 3430, 3604, 3748, 3756, 3759, 3960 & 4124	D3261, 08187, 08188, 08189, 08190, 08191, 08192, 08193, 08194, 08195, 08198, 08349, 08350, 08351, 08352, 08484, 08580, 08581, 08593, 08779 & 08835
25	7502, 7514, 7619 & 25031	None
31	None	31102, 31166 & 31170
37	6916, 6930, 6934, 6939, 6944, 6973, 6990, 6992, 6997 & 37179	37138, 37139, 37162, 37189, 37207, 37223, 37225, 37228, 37247, 37251, 37255, 37256, 37269, 37274, 37275, 37276, 37280, 37282, 37286, 37288, 37290 & 37292
45–46	115 & 45111	45021, 45025, 46016, 46020 & 46043
47	1105, 1559, 1569, 1603, 1606, 1652, 1669, 1685, 1688, 1694, 1708, 1711, 1735, 1752, 1755, 1802, 1813, 1816, 1884, 1902, 1903, 1909, 1910, 47069 & 47247	47002, 47029, 47030, 47054, 47059, 47061, 47070, 47081, 47082, 47094, 47103, 47105, 47106, 47147, 47231, 47234, 47236, 47239, 47241, 47246, 47251, 47339, 47344, 47366, 47377, 47381 & 47424
52	1051 & 1067	None

TRACTION MAINTENANCE DEPOTS

Above & below: Two images from the 1970s that involve the footbridge from De Crouche Place. Firstly, on Saturday 26 February 1977, the bridge was busy, mainly with spotters, but also one or two BR employees. In the three reception sidings beyond the bridge are 47060, 37178 and 37280. Locomotives would be parked there before they were moved west to the rear of the refuelling shed which is to the right of this view. In the background smoke can be seen belching from Cardiff East Moors Steelworks. The second photograph shows the "classic" view from the footbridge on 13 May 1978, with 33025 being a rare visitor at the time. Class 33s would become much more common in the 1980s, when they were assigned to the trains between Portsmouth Harbour and Cardiff, and later from Cardiff to Crewe and Manchester.

Wales

Above: It was very unusual to see a Class 50 in the depot at Canton, let alone in the heavy maintenance shed. The class were usually looked after at Laira and Bristol Bath Road depots. On 1 October 1977, 50043 needed attention at Canton and is seen at the eastern end of the heavy maintenance building.

Above: Class 45s and Class 46s were common at Canton, visiting on passenger services from Manchester, Newcastle and Leeds. On 1 January 1977, 45057 and 46016 stand in the refuelling shed. The indifference of the staff to the photographer was a feature of many depots during the 1970s and 1980s.

TRACTION MAINTENANCE DEPOTS

Above: At the southern edge of the 30-acre Canton complex was an eight-track carriage shed which housed the large diesel multiple unit (DMU) fleet that operated on the nearby Valley Lines and the coaching stock for trains to Crewe, Manchester, Leeds and Newcastle. On 18 October 1977, 25221 stands at the front of the stock for a Crewe service with several DMUs stabled beside it.

Below: This view shows Canton depot from its western end on 29 October 1977, with 20 or so members of Classes 08, 37 and 47 scattered across the sidings. On the far left is the SWML, then the three-road refuelling shed and on the right is the four-road heavy maintenance building.

Wales

Above: On 27 December 1977, just after the Christmas shut down period (no trains at all ran on Christmas Day or Boxing Day), Canton was packed with 79 locomotives. Among these were 46035, 37279 and 45001 which all pose at the eastern end of the maintenance shed.

Above: Unusually a line of Class 08 shunters were stored inside the refuelling depot at Canton during the Christmas week. On the evening of 27 December 1977, 08593, 08589, 08195, 08193 and 08189 were all found above the inspection pit there.

TRACTION MAINTENANCE DEPOTS

Above: Three of Canton's Class 47s are seen undergoing maintenance at the depot on 6 January 1978. From left to right are 47143, 47225 and 47251.

Above: This locomotive portrait has special significance for me. It was taken on 23 May 1978 after a friend telephoned to tip me off that a Class 40 was on the depot at Canton. I was revising for my A-levels and hopped on my Honda C70 moped to take this picture of 40182. On the way home I was knocked off my moped and suffered a broken left shoulder. Being left-handed, this led to me having to dictate all my A-level exams that summer!

Wales

Above: On 20 June 1979 the maintenance shed is almost full of locomotives receiving major overhauls. From left to right are 47254, 47377, 47087, 47121 and 46028.

Above: On 8 May 1982, 33014 and 33063 stand at the front of rakes of coaching stock within the carriage shed. 33014 will take a train to Crewe and 33063 will head in a different direction by working 2O61, the 17.20 Cardiff Central–Weymouth as far as Bristol Temple Meads.

TRACTION MAINTENANCE DEPOTS

Above: On 1 June 1982, the consecutively numbered 56051 and 56052 stand at the western end of the main maintenance shed at Canton alongside 37231. In the background, the crane that was used when locomotives needed their wheelsets to be changed can be seen rising up.

Above: This general view of the east end of Canton fuelling shed was taken on 28 December 1985. From left to right are 45136, 45012, 56061, 31165 and 47310.

Above: On 11 January 1992, less than 12 months since it had entered service, 60033 enjoys some natural light in the most photogenic bay of Canton's heavy maintenance shed, when nothing was obscuring its western end.

Left: The fleet of Class 03s with cut down cabs that operated on the Burry Port and Gwendraeth Valley line were allocated to Swansea's Landore depot and usually stabled at Llanelli during weekends. Occasionally one of the small shunters could be found on Canton if it needed attention from the wheel lathe there. This photograph of 03382 was taken during June 1982, when it was likely to be visiting for that reason, as its coupling rods have been removed and the far wheel is resting on a wheel skate, suggesting a wheel flat. I decided to pose for this image, as it was taken by a fellow medical student from Oxford who had confessed an interest in railways and popped over to Cardiff for a weekend shed bash.

TRACTION MAINTENANCE DEPOTS

Above: During the sectorisation era, the motive power that could be seen at Canton began to change as many of the more powerful Class 56s and 60s that were allocated there began to replace the older types. On 27 December 1992, 60054 and 37054 were found undergoing major repairs.

Below: It was a full house at Canton on 27 December 1992 due to the Christmas shutdown period. Even though more than 50 locomotives were on shed that day, only 60065, 37882, 37272 and 56073 are identifiable in this photograph, as a consequence of the modern practice of placing the locomotive number on the cab end.

Below right: By the summer of 1997, it was all change at Canton as the privatised train operating companies had begun to arrive. On the right, 37427 displays the new red and yellow EWS livery, which remarkably can still be seen on a handful of main line freight locos today, even though it has now been defunct for many years. On the left, 60080 and two Class 37s are in the much shorter-lived Transrail livery.

Wales

Above: Whilst these final two views of Cardiff Canton show the depot slightly outside the timeframe of this volume, they have been included because they show some of the changes that took place during the 1990s. One reason that I took far fewer shed shots after 1992, was the increased security that sprung up at depots. I was horrified to arrive at my favourite footbridge at Canton depot on 20 August 1996 and find that the usual stroll round the depot had been rendered impossible by this new security gate. The locomotives seen behind the gate include 37111, 37799, 37802, 56001, 56016, 56076 and 60035. Palisade fencing and much stricter security really spoilt what had been an innocent and pretty safe pastime for decades.

TRACTION MAINTENANCE DEPOTS

Above: On 20 May 1978, 08352 and 08194 were found stabled at Cardiff East Dock. At the time, there were 18 regular duties for Cardiff Canton's shunting locomotives, six of which were based in and around Cardiff Docks. Usually four of the locomotives posted across Cardiff Docks would be stabled at Tidal Sidings and the other two, which are seen here, would be near to the 125-lever North East Junction signal box which closed in 1980.

Below and opposite page: In the 1970s Radyr was the hub for coal traffic from over a dozen collieries and was the starting point for the many trip workings that travelled up the various Valley Lines on an hourly basis. The old steam shed illustrated in the first image was used to stable diesels during the 1960s, but had become disused by the 1970s. The adjacent permanent way depot housed PWM651, a departmental shunting locomotive that pottered back and forth on the sidings there for most of its life. The aerial view was taken from the entrance to Radyr Comprehensive School and shows five Class 37s, an 08 and PWM651 stabled in the yard at Radyr during 1977. This was a typical number of locomotives for a weekday, but there could be up to 15 stabled there during the weekends. The site of the stabling point and yard are now occupied by a housing estate and the view from the school is obscured by foliage.

Wales

TRACTION MAINTENANCE DEPOTS

Above: During the 1970s there would be up to five locomotives stabled at Aberdare, adjacent to the town's long closed High Level station. By 1982, when this image was taken, Mountain Ash pit had closed and there were usually just a couple of Class 37s present. The two examples found on 13 December 1982 were 37239 and 37214.

Above: On 30 December 1983 three of the pairs of 37s used on Merry-go-round (MGR) traffic to the nearby Aberthaw Power Station were stabled at Barry. On the left are 37285 & 37275 and to their right are 37282, 37287, 37302 and 37234. The old steam depot there was used predominantly to repair MGR wagons, whilst the locomotives that worked the coal trains were usually stabled outside, to the south of the steam shed, as is the case here.

Right: This elevated view was taken after climbing a lighting mast in the semi-derelict sorting sidings of Margam Hump Yard on Christmas Day in 1983. It provides a good overview of Margam depot, showing how the locos stabled there were spread over a wide area during the holiday period. A row of six Class 37s, headed by 37296, has been parked in the most westerly sorting siding. More 37s can be made out in the distance, with another row of six 37s seen above the depot roof and two more locos to the left of the building, near Margam Sorting Sidings signal box.

Above: 37803 & 37701 are seen stabled at Barry on 22 December 1992, with fellow heavyweight class members 37796 & 37896 and 08668 visible behind 37701. The shunter's duties included moving the vehicles that received attention in Barry's wagon repair shops and hauling the twice-daily trip working into the nearby docks.

MARGAM

The depot at Margam was almost impossible to visit without a car because it was a 90-minute walk from Port Talbot station, a distance of over five miles! There was however, a bus for railway staff which could be used by prior arrangement. Because of the depot's remoteness though, I did not visit it until I had a car. In my experience, the staff were invariably friendly and allowed visitors to take pictures. The depot was built in 1961 as part of the new hump yard complex at Margam; it had a three-road shed and was responsible for around 50 locomotives. It continued to service freight and shunting locomotives until its closure in 2009, when the stabling of locomotives was moved to a new single-track shed adjacent to Margam Knuckle Yard. The buildings were demolished in 2012 and today it is difficult to see where the shed once stood as the area has returned to nature.

TRACTION MAINTENANCE DEPOTS

Above: At the north end of a fairly full Margam depot on 23 July 1983, from left to right, are 47066, 45064, 37247, 47246, 08361 and 47057 with two classmates.

Above: On 11 August 1978, 37159 and 47048 stand inside the main shed at Margam. At this time the hump yard was still operational, although the hump would close in 1980 and the yard was then rapidly rationalised and eventually replaced by a refurbished Margam Knuckle Yard in 1987.

Wales

Above: 56037 "Richard Trevithick" rests outside the shed at Margam on 27 May 1983. Three other 56s stand behind it, forming the two pairs of 56s that operated daily on the Port Talbot to Llanwern iron ore trains.

TRACTION MAINTENANCE DEPOTS

Above: On 28 December 1985, the low winter sun highlights a packed Margam depot. Closest to the camera are 37238 and 47148.

Above right and right: A little outside the date range for this book, these images show the transition in motive power during the last decade at Margam. They are also testament to how the depot remained one of the most friendly sites during the privatisation era, when so many other depots became strictly out of bounds for visiting enthusiasts. The first, taken on 17 February 1999, shows 59202 (which was used on iron ore trains for a short spell), with 66088 to its left and 56033 to the right. Among the other locomotives on shed is an unidentified Rail Express Systems Class 47, providing a reminder of the parcels traffic that operated at the time from Carmarthen and Swansea. The second image, taken on 26 July 2000, is dominated by Class 60s, after a fleet of these had been transferred to the area to handle the iron ore and steel traffic in South Wales. From left to right are 66008, a partially visible unidentified 66, 67025 (used on parcels traffic), 60016, 60071 and 60098.

LANDORE

The depot was a 20-minute walk from Swansea station and was not one I visited often. This was mainly because most of the motive power that was serviced there also passed through Cardiff at some stage. That just left the depot's

Class	Locos on 3 April 1975	Locos on 26 December 1983
03	03141, 03144 & 03145	03119, 03120, 03141, 03142, 03144, 03145, 03151, 03152 & 03382
08	08577, 08591, 08656 & 08660	08259, 08394, 08400, 08592, 08649, 08653, 08660, 08662, 08663, 08664, 08818 & 08898
33	None	33021, 33027 & 33033
37	37175, 37176, 37180, 37182, 37183, 37192, 37206, 37207 & 37306	37240, 37294 & 37307
43	None	43011, 43030, 43128 & 43166
46	46051	None
47	47015, 47033, 47091, 47119, 47121, 47142, 47240, 47356, 47407, 47452, 47456, 47465, 47472, 47477, 47484, 47487, 47490, 47494, 47496, 47497, 47500, 47503, 47504, 47507, 47510, 47514, 47530, 47538 & 47540	47012, 47143, 47157, 47465, 47510, 47520, 47551 & 47557
52	1037	None

Table 2: The locos that were present at Landore on two dates in 1975 and 1983.

TRACTION MAINTENANCE DEPOTS

shunting locomotives to track down and this could be done by visiting the stabling points that were linked to Landore, leaving little incentive to visit the depot itself. The stabling points were dotted around West Wales and included Llanelli, Carmarthen, Pantyffynon, Swansea East Dock and Swansea Carriage Sidings. Landore depot opened in 1963 and was similar in design to that at Cardiff Canton. There was a four-road heavy maintenance shed with room for eight locomotives and a three-road servicing and refuelling shed with space for another six engines. The table on page 26 gives an idea of the volume and variety of motive power that could be seen at Landore.

Above: On Boxing Day in 1983 the staff allowed me to wander round a packed Landore depot. A quick nip up one of the lighting masts enabled me to capture this view of the large array of shunters allocated to the depot. The full list of locos that were on shed that day can be seen in Table 2.

Above right & right: These two images of the depot were also taken on Boxing Day 1983. Looking south west into the low winter sun, with the maintenance building on the left, the first view includes some of the Class 03s that were normally stabled at Bury Port or Llanelli. These have been moved to Landore for the festive period. To the right is the three-track fuelling shed, one road of which has a full High Speed Train (HST) set parked in it. In the second image, which looks in the other direction, the fuelling and servicing shed is seen in the centre, with the maintenance building to the right. At least ten of the 21 shunting locomotives that were present that day are visible.

Wales

TRACTION MAINTENANCE DEPOTS

Above top, above, above right and right: These four images were taken on a sunny 22 September 1984 and show a variety of everyday activity at Landore depot. A member of staff is at work cleaning 37300 outside, while others attend to 37210, 37251 & 37240 inside the main maintenance shed. The inspection building contained Metro-Cammell Class 101 set C805 that day, which consisted of vehicles 51462 & 51530, while 08191 and 08400 are at rest outside. Note the builders plate beneath the number of 08191, stating that it was built in 1956 at Derby and the unofficial decal which I think says "Wales is best"!

Wales

TRACTION MAINTENANCE DEPOTS

Above: Landore depot had two major stabling points, Swansea East Dock and Llanelli. During the 1970s, the latter was kept busy with local coal and steel traffic, as well as being the stabling point for the locomotives that worked on the former Burry Port and Gwendraeth Valley Railway. This view from the west end of the old goods shed at Llanelli on 18 June 1982 finds 47150 and 47408 at rest, while 08400 arrives from the west before it is stabled inside the goods shed.

Below left: During the late 1970s and early 1980s, the Class 03s that were used on the former Burry Port & Gwendraeth Valley Railway would be stabled at Llanelli over the weekend. Such was the case on 24 March 1983 when 03145, 03152, 03144, 03382 & 03119 were all found at the old goods shed which had become the locomotive stabling point in the 1970s. The section of the mineral line that had the tightest clearances closed later in 1983, which led to the 03s being replaced by reduced height Class 08s.

Above: This second image of the stabling point at Llanelli on 24 March 1983 shows 47035, 37300 and 47227, as well as the five Class 03s in the background. The traction required for the freight services that worked on the Cynheidre branch and from the nearby Trostre Tinplate Works usually meant that two or three main line locomotives would be stabled in the goods yard.

Above: By 3 July 1986, the 03s with cut down cabs that worked on the branch to the north of Pembrey & Burry Port had been replaced by specially modified Class 08s. In the foreground 08991 is stabled at Llanelli and its reduced cab height is very evident in this head on view, especially when contrasted to that of 08191 in the background.

Above: Pantyffynon lies 12 miles north-west of Llanelli, on the southernmost part of the Central Wales Line. On an average weekend five Class 37s and a single 08 could be found stabled there, whilst on weekdays the number of locomotives present would rarely be more than two because most were out at work. On Friday 18 June 1982 I was fortunate to find 37279, 37251 and 37239 all stabled in the yard at Pantyffynon.

EBBW JUNCTION

My notes record very few formal visits to Ebbw Junction, quite simply because it was a 45-minute walk from Newport station and the numbers of the locos on the depot could often be collected whilst passing by on the SWML. The diesel depot opened in 1966 after it was decided that the old Ebbw Junction steam shed could not be repurposed as a diesel depot. It had a fairly short life, closing in 1982 as part of some wider changes in the region, including the closure of Ebbw Vale Steelworks, the collapse of South Wales' coal traffic and the contraction of the docks in Newport. One of the buildings was reopened as a permanent way depot, but as one of our images shows, this was demolished in April 1995. Stabling points linked to Ebbw Junction included Newport Pill, which was deep within the docks, Aberbeeg up the Ebbw Vale valley and Severn Tunnel Junction. Severn Tunnel Junction was by far the largest stabling point and outlasted its parent depot by five years. After Ebbw Junction closed in 1982, many of the locomotives that previously stabled there used the sidings at Newport Godfrey Road instead.

Class	Locos on 10 August 1974	Locos on 8 October 1977
08	08029, 08109, 08122, 08135, 08582, 08595, 08647, 08657, 08846, 08848, 08853, 08894 & 08940	08029, 08110, 08634, 08639, 08652, 08801 & 08822
11	None	12071
25	25030, 25031, 25059, 25063, 25153, 25156, 25157, 25158, 25159, 25161, 25163, 25165, 25166 & 25219	None
37	37203, 37220, 37222, 37231, 37233, 37284, 37290 & 37308	37138, 37159, 37196, 37213, 37217, 37230, 37233, 37234, 37238, 37251, 37269, 37270 & 37294
47	Brush Prototype D1200 & 47365	None

Table 3: The locos present at Ebbw Junction on two dates in the mid-1970s.

Wales

Below: The Brush prototype D1200 "Falcon" spent the end of its working life allocated to Ebbw Junction. It is seen here on 10 August 1974, displaying its regular headcode of 9E61, indicating that it had been working the local trip freights hauling steel products between Alexandra Dock Junction, Llanwern, Newport Docks and the Uskmouth branch. Behind it is 25161, one of 14 Class 25s on the depot that day and 47365, an interloper from the Midlands. The full list of locomotives on the depot that Saturday is summarised in Table 3.

Above: On 24 September 1977, having just acquired a Honda C70 moped, I made a quick visit to Ebbw Junction and found 37196, 37210, 37222 and 37289 stabled at the south end of the shed.

TRACTION MAINTENANCE DEPOTS

Above: This alternative view of Ebbw Junction on 24 September 1977 shows another four of the 20 or so locomotives that were stabled there. From left to right are 37252, 08582, 08029 and 08657.

Below, above right and right: These three images were all taken on 8 October 1977 and give a good impression of how Ebbw Junction looked on a typical Saturday during the 1970s. A complete list of the locomotives found on the depot that day is given in Table 3.

Wales

TRACTION MAINTENANCE DEPOTS

Above: This photograph was taken on 7 April 1995 when I made a brief visit back to the UK from Australia and was surprised to find demolition well underway at Ebbw Junction. Although there is still a Network Rail facility on the site, much of the land that the depot used to occupy has since been redeveloped and is now covered by housing.

Above: The sidings at Newport Godfrey Road were immediately west of Newport's station. On 28 May 1988 they were full, with from left to right 37207, 37690, 37146, 37142 and 37032 in the far siding. In the next siding is an unidentified Class 37 and then 37698, 37275 and 47287. The next row the contains two 08s and a 47, and 37133 and 37696 complete the scene on the far right. The sidings here dated back 100 years but were at their busiest between 1982 and the early 2000s. They eventually closed in 2006 and were then lifted to allow expansion of the station car park.

SEVERN TUNNEL JUNCTION

The six-road steam depot at Severn Tunnel Junction was replaced by a single-track diesel servicing depot nearer to the adjacent marshalling yards in 1966. Originally a handful of Class 08s were allocated there, but these were soon transferred to Ebbw Junction and Severn Tunnel Junction was reclassified as a stabling point for the main depot at Ebbw Junction. From 1968, six of the 08s allocated to Ebbw Junction were outstationed at Severn Tunnel Junction. The 1986 South Wales Freight Review proposed that Severn Tunnel Junction and its associated marshalling yards should close. These had been such a busy rail location and so pivotal to South Wales' freight traffic that I could hardly believe the announcement when I heard it on the national news in 1986, however, they did close in November 1987. The building that previously serviced locomotives still stands, but it is no longer rail connected.

Below: On 12 June 1983 this view was captured from half-way up a lighting mast, to the west of the shed at Severn Tunnel Junction and shows 37301, 47337 and 37273 nearest the camera. Further back, the front ends of 47156 and 37285 are visible, behind which further locomotives are stabled.

TRACTION MAINTENANCE DEPOTS

Above & below: These two images were taken on Friday 5 August 1983, when two Class 40s visited the stabling point. The class were commonplace at Severn Tunnel Junction between 1982 and 1985, when they were responsible for many of the mixed freight workings from Mossend, Carlisle and Warrington. They replaced electric locomotives on the unelectrified portion of the journey from Crewe to Newport via Hereford. Firstly, 25212 (left) and 40044 stand at the west end of the sidings alongside a variety of Class 37s. 40044 had arrived on a mixed freight from Warrington Arpley Yard earlier that day and would return north on the Monday morning with 8M18, the mixed freight to Arpley. In the second view, which looks in the opposite direction, 40044 is visible in the centre (to the right of the long line of 37s) and 40035 can be seen in front of the building on the right. 40035 had arrived at Cardiff Tidal Sidings earlier in the day with 6Z80, a special air-braked freight from Mossend and it was being refuelled, ready to take the 18.10 departure to Mossend. 40044 sits among 12 Class 37s to its left, another 37 on the same line, a 31 & 45 to its right and finally a solitary Class 08 inside the refuelling shed.

Wales

Above & below: These two pictures illustrate further visits of Class 40s to Severn Tunnel Junction and were taken on 24 April 1984. 40013 "ANDANIA" is stabled adjacent to the station, having arrived from Carlisle Kingmoor with a mixed freight. The second view shows 40181 alongside 37080 and 45026. Typically, traffic to and from the South Wales hinterland was handled by Class 37s, whilst traffic from Tinsley and the North East usually employed "foreign" Class 37s (often split headcode examples) and that from Toton and Bescot utilised Class 45s and sometimes Class 20s.

TRACTION MAINTENANCE DEPOTS

Above: This image from 29 July 1985 gives an idea of how busy Severn Tunnel Junction used to be. 47100 has just arrived with a Speedlink freight from Eastleigh to Severn Tunnel Junction, while examples of Classes 47, 37 and 08 can be seen at work in the Up and Down Yards, and a light engine Class 47 passes on the main line. On the right, the stabling point contains at least ten different 37s, a 47, a 25, two Class 45s and an 08.

Right: Before Severn Tunnel Junction depot closed it was hard to imagine there being no freight trains there. I only made a single visit between its closure in 1987 and 2015, on 28 May 1988, in order to record this image of the decimation that had taken place. I don't know how much the abolition of the yards and depot was due to the planned second River Severn road bridge, but I suspect it was a major factor.

Wales

Class	Locos
08	08844, 08848 & 08932
25	25020, 25185 & 25254
31	31265
37	37181, 37192, 37225, 37253, 37285, 37303 & 37304
46	46047
47	47087, 47091, 47227, 47232 & 47509
52	1028, 1043 & 1047

Table 4: The locos present at Seven Tunnel Junction on 14 December 1974.

SCOTLAND

INVERNESS

The depot at Inverness was only a five-minute walk from the station and was perhaps one of the friendliest on the network, as one or two of the illustrations in this section imply. The depot wasn't altered much to accommodate main line diesels when they began arriving from early 1960. The old Lochgorm Railway Works building was used for diesel maintenance and a small refuelling facility was installed at the Rose Street end of the site. Although main line diesels all but disappeared from 1995, today the depot continues to service coaching stock and DMUs after the facilities were extensively rebuilt in 2008/9.

Class	Locos on 16 August 1976	Locos on 4 September 1979
08	08620	08728
20	None	20080, 20085 & 20102
24–25	24118	25239 & 25240
26	26010, 26011, 26012, 26018, 26021, 26022, 26026, 26027, 26029, 26033, 26037, 26038, 26039, 26044, 26045 & 26046	26014, 26018, 26023, 26024, 26035, 26036 & 26040
40	40123	40151
47	47469	47120, 47274 & 47546

‖ **Table 5:** The locomotives that were present at Inverness on two days during the 1970s.

‖ **Above:** One of my favourite depot images is this view of 26032 in the old Lochgorm Works building at Inverness on the morning of 12 August 1976. The madness of those days can be encapsulated in a few of my travel details. I had left my home station, Cardiff, at 22.50 on 10 August to travel to Sheffield, arriving there at 06.11 the next morning. From there, a day of shed bashing ensued as I progressively made my way north with visits to the depots at York, Darlington, Thornaby, Shildon, Sunderland and Gateshead. I then left Newcastle at 21.03, to arrive in Edinburgh at 22.58, where I proceeded to sleep on the station platform for a few hours until I departed for Aberdeen at 04.03. It may have been the summer of 1976, but it was freezing on the platform! From Aberdeen, I continued to Inverness, arriving there at 10.19, where I found 08620 and a healthy contingent of Class 26s in the form of 26011, 26012, 26018, 26020, 26022, 26029, 26032, 26037, 26038, 26039, 26041, 26042 & 26046.

‖ **Above right:** This photograph was taken at Inverness depot on the morning of 13 September 1979. 40066 stands adjacent to the signal box on the southern side of the depot that had the curious name of "Loco Box". The box had 40 levers when it opened in 1896 and this was increased to 64 levers in 1904. It eventually closed after more than 90 years of service when Inverness was resignalled in 1987.

Scotland

Above: Again, on 13 September 1979, 20020 and sister locomotive 20085 take a breather on the depot while they await their turn at the refuelling point after having just arrived with the Elgin to Inverness Milburn Yard empty tank train.

TRACTION MAINTENANCE DEPOTS

Scotland

This page & opposite: Table 5 lists the locomotives seen at the depot on two dates that were just over three years apart. On the second of these, 4 September 1979, the traction bore some similarities and some differences to that found at Inverness depot three years earlier. In the first view, from left to right are 25240, 26036, 26014 and 20102 & 20080 with 40151 perched behind them. The second general view shows 26018 & 26033 outside the old Lochgorm Works building. We then have a closeup of 20102 & 20080 being refuelled by one member of depot staff, while another is at work cleaning the windows after the pair arrived with a fuel oil train bound for RAF Lossiemouth near Elgin. That is followed by a moment that captures some other depot staff chatting and joking as they walk past 20085, 26024 and 26036.

TRACTION MAINTENANCE DEPOTS

Above: 47274 finally gets its turn at the refuelling point in Inverness on 4 September 1979, having arrived with an overnight freight from Millerhill, while 26035 stands to its left.

Below: Loco Box signal box is seen from an alternative angle to that illustrated earlier, with 26013 standing outside the old Lochgorm Works buildings on 5 September 1979.

Scotland

Above: On 14 August 1982, 27007 and 47467 stand at the end of the inspection pit roads in the old Lochgorm Works building at Inverness. The other locos that were present within the building that day were 08568, 25234, 25247 and 26046.

Above: 20215 & 20107 had arrived overnight with another fuel oil train from Grangemouth and are now seen refuelling at Inverness depot on 5 September 1979.

Above: Looking down on the Lochgorm Works building, with its modern corrugated roof, finds 27019 & 27040 backing into the station before they take a train south to Glasgow Queen Street on 14 August 1982. I had never noticed before, but this photograph catches an eager rail enthusiast dashing across the goods yard tracks to get a picture of the pair!

Above: On 14 August 1982, 26046 and 25247 are amongst several other locomotives undergoing repairs inside the old Works buildings at Inverness diesel depot.

Right: 08828 shunts a single VDA van containing locomotive spare parts within the confines of Ferryhill depot on 24 March 1981. Three Class 40s flank the shunter, but sadly their numbers were not recorded.

ABERDEEN FERRYHILL

Aberdeen Ferryhill was a 25-minute walk from Aberdeen station. The depot dated back to 1850 and became a diesel facility when steam in the area came to an end in 1966. Ferryhill was closed as a depot in 1988 and has since been taken over by the Ferryhill Railway Heritage Trust which formed in 2007 and has restored the turntable there. From 1988, diesel locomotives were stabled in the goods yard to the east of Aberdeen station, but this closed in 2000 and the site is now occupied by a shopping centre and car park. There is a depot on the west side of the station and this is where Scotrail's High Speed Trains and multiple units are now serviced.

Class	Locos
06	06006
08	08443, 08515, 08710 & 08817

Table 6: The locos that were present at Aberdeen Ferryhill on 11 August 1976.

Above: On 27 July 1988, just weeks after Ferryhill closed, 37009 & 37046 are seen at the new stabling and fuelling point on the western edge of Guild Street Goods Depot. This area is now occupied by a shopping centre and car park.

TRACTION MAINTENANCE DEPOTS

Above: This general view of Ferryhill depot on 24 March 1981 gives a better idea of its size and the variety of traction that it would host, as examples of five different main line diesel classes were present that day.

Above: On 11 August 1976 a visit to Ferryhill depot yielded the sighting of 06006, which is pictured here alongside 08515. The Class 06 was used on trip workings to the nearby harbour. Only one of the 10-strong class was allocated to Aberdeen; the others were allocated to Townhill, Dundee and Eastfield depots.

Above right: On 11 August 1976 26023 is seen stabled alongside a Class 101 set that includes vehicle 56399 at Dundee West. Also on shed that day were 06005, 08276, 08426, 27015, 27016, 47207 and a variety of motor vehicles that seem to have reached the end of their lives!

Right: On 20 June 1981, the holding sidings to the west of Perth station contain four of the Scottish Region's Type 2s in the form of 26010, 26011, 26044 and 27010.

Scotland

DUNDEE

The depot was a ten-minute walk from Dundee station and like with most Scottish depots in the 1970s, access was usually easy and the staff were friendly. The former steam depot at Dundee West was converted to service DMUs and opened in 1960. It had an allocation of shunting locomotives and was also used to stable main line diesels. Its importance was short-lived however and DMU servicing was moved elsewhere during the 1970s and early 1980s. It had lost its locomotive allocation by 1982 and the buildings were eventually demolished in 1987. A major stabling point for Dundee was Perth, where facilities for locomotives to stable were set up to the west of the station in 1970, after the steam depot at Perth closed. Although the sidings that were used to stable locomotives in the 1970s have now been removed, there is still a refuelling and inspection shed to the west of Perth station and the old carriage sidings are used to service the DMU fleet now used on Inverness and Aberdeen services. A visit to Perth on 13 August 1976 found the following present: 08725, 08736, 20089, 20225, 25033, 25083, 25096, 26013, 37033, 40158 and 40162. The number of locomotives reflects the importance of Perth during the 1970s, when it usually held more locomotives than its "parent" depot at Dundee.

TRACTION MAINTENANCE DEPOTS

DUNFERMLINE TOWNHILL

Townhill diesel depot opened in 1970, when it took on the work of the former Thornton Junction depot using buildings that previously housed Dunfermline's wagon works. The site was difficult to reach without a car as it was a 50-minute walk from Dunfermline Town station. Consequently, I didn't visit the depot until 1976 when I spent virtually the whole day exploring Townhill and the neighbouring Thornton Yard. Thornton Yard also opened in 1970 when Thornton Junction depot closed and was used to refuel locomotives on the frequent freight trains to and from the hump yard at Thornton. That day in 1976 was notable for getting lost in Methil Docks looking for a shunter and then being offered a lift back to Thornton Yard by the crew of 24115, before being allowed to ride in the railway workers' bus back to Kirkcaldy station. Without this assistance I doubt I would ever have got back to Edinburgh that night! In 1980 I was able to borrow the family VW camper van for a week so I could take pictures for my first book "Freight Trains of British Rail" which was published in 1982. That was the only time that I took any photos of Townhill depot and the stabling point at Thornton Yard. Things came full circle in 1984 when Townhill closed and its locomotives were transferred to Thornton Yard where a new two-track servicing shed was built. The collapse of both coal and general freight traffic then led to this new depot being quite short-lived and it closed in 1992. It saw a brief revival under EWS but had been demolished by 2013.

Scotland

Above: The weekend line-up at Townhill depot on 28 June 1980 is summarised in Table 7. Most of the Class 20s that were present are visible in this view, along with 25011 on the right. All the locomotives were stabled outside the former wagon works building which was locked.

Class	Locos on 12 August 1976	Locos on 28 June 1980
06	06002 & 06009	None
08	08145, 08341 & 08445	08175, 08425, 08570, 08726
20	20184, 20216, 20218, 20221, 20226 & 20227	20191, 20201, 20203, 20206, 20216, 20217, 20221, 20222, 20223, 20224 & 20227
24/25	24112	25011

Table 7: The locos that were present at Dunfermline Townhill on two different dates.

Above: Also on 28 June 1980, the fuelling point at Thornton yard is full of locomotives that were stabled for the weekend. On the left are 25065 and 25019 with 20225, 20205, 20202, 20049, 20111 and 20184 for company. 08271 was also present that day and is out of shot.

Above: On 17 August 1990, after I had accompanied the crew on a trip freight working from Thornton to Crombie and Rosyth Dockyard, the depot at Thornton was busier. On the right, 26026 is stabled, ready to work a local ballast trip and 20124 & 20138 await their next duty which would be the 7L22 freight to Mossend. In the yard on the left 08761 busies itself with a bit of shunting, whilst 20137 & 20118 stand on the 6G07 arrival from Rosyth Dockyard.

Above: On 17 August 1990, 08761 in Scotrail livery shunts a rake of MGR wagons into the two-road diesel depot at Thornton Yard. In its later years the site was mainly used for wagon repairs, rather than diesel maintenance.

TRACTION MAINTENANCE DEPOTS

Above: On 9 August 1991, 37693 waits at the exit of the Westfield Colliery branch (which is also visible in the photograph of 08761) with a coal train for Longannet Power Station. The depot at Thornton Yard otherwise looks a bit unused, with 26024 to the left of the 37 and 26008 (which worked a trip to Cameron Bridge that day) to the left of the shed. The edge of 08761 can just be glimpsed in the centre.

Above: A Class 06, originally allocated to Dundee and then to Townhill, was always out-stabled at Markinch to work the Auchmuty branch which ran east from Markinch. The small shunter was needed as the clearances on the line were very restricted. On 28 June 1980, 06003 was found stabled in the goods yard there.

Scotland

GRANGEMOUTH

Grangemouth depot was a 30-minute walk from Falkirk Grahamston station and on my several visits to it I found that access was always easy. Grangemouth effectively became a diesel depot in 1965 when it lost its steam allocation, although very few physical alterations were ever made to the original steam shed. It serviced the freight locomotives that worked from the extensive yards in Grangemouth Docks and in later years from the refineries at Grangemouth. There were plans to build a new modern diesel depot on the site in the late 1980s but traffic collapsed when Speedlink ended in 1991 and the depot closed in 1993. The buildings were eventually demolished in 2000.

Above: On the evening of Saturday 8 July 1978 the depot at Grangemouth was full. This overall view shows the variety of traction that was found there, which from left to right consists of 37146, 20046, 08505, 40168, 25044, 20122 and 37149. Another six locomotives were also present and these were 08175, 08722, 20123, 20207, 25009 and 27024.

TRACTION MAINTENANCE DEPOTS

Above: Nearly eight years after the previous photograph was taken, on 27 April 1986, 27207 and 27058 stand inside the main shed at Grangemouth depot, which dates back to the steam era.

Scotland

Opposite bottom, left & below: These three views of Grangemouth depot were captured on 30 March 1989. 20145 & 20185 stand beside 37245 while they are serviced and refuelled before their next duty, which will be the evening Speedlink service to Mossend. That lunchtime, 26014 was found within the single track maintenance building at Grangemouth as it undergoes light repairs. Finally, a view that was taken later in the afternoon from just inside the main shed shows 37023, with 37097 & 08620 in the distance and the end of 37245 on the left. 08620 had been engaged in shunting at the adjacent Blue Circle cement terminal.

TRACTION MAINTENANCE DEPOTS

HAYMARKET

A 15-minute walk from Haymarket station and even closer to the Youth Hostel in Edinburgh, Haymarket was a friendly depot that was easy to wander round. The depot was a piecemeal conversion from the original steam shed, with a new roof added and facilities to service main line diesels. Steam finished at Haymarket in 1963, after which the depot looked after the main line diesels that worked services to Inverness, Aberdeen, Glasgow and London. When HSTs were introduced on Edinburgh to King's Cross services in the late 1970s, their maintenance was transferred to Craigentinny depot on the other side of Edinburgh and this continued until the HSTs were withdrawn from the route in 2019. In more recent years the depot has been responsible for a large DMU fleet, although it was updated when it received an allocation of Scotrail's newly refurbished HST sets when they were introduced in 2018 and it continues to be a busy depot today. A typical line up at the depot in the mid-1970s is shown in Table 8.

Class	Locos on 20 April 1974	Locos on 9 July 1978
08	3316 & 08720	08565, 08711 & 08755
20	8039 & 20078	20201 & 20220
24–25	24065, 24072 & 25215	25023, 25037, 25075, 25087 & 25091
26	26004, 26006, 26015, 26017 & 26020	26005, 26036 & 26037
27	5391, 27101, 27114, 27117 & 27118	27012, 27103, 27108, 27110, 27207 & 27210
40	40061, 40159, 40161 & 40165	40062, 40066, 40101, 40123, 40142, 40164, 40165 & 40173
46	46030, 46031, 46039 & 46041	46029, 46031 & 46048
47	1973, 1975, 1976, 47003, 47053, 47135, 47160, 47268, 47413, 47435 & 47458	47271, 47428, 47461, 47467, 47469 & 47516
55	None	55013, 55019 & 55022

Table 8: The locos that were present at Haymarket on two dates during the 1970s.

There were two stabling points linked to Haymarket depot, the nearby Waverley station and the small diesel depot at Millerhill Marshalling Yard. The latter opened in 1962, with a single track servicing shed and was used to service freight locomotives until 2016 when it closed and was demolished. Table 9 gives a sample of the motive power to be found at Millerhill during a typical weekend in the 1970s.

Class	Locos
08	08246, 08575, 08717, 08734 & 08789
24–25	24094 & 24104
26	26001, 26002, 26006 & 26007
27	27011
40	40078 & 40154

Table 9: The locos that were present at Millerhill on 14 August 1976.

Below: First thing in the morning on 15 August 1976 and 55020 and 55014 stand alongside 25012 outside Haymarket's main maintenance shed. The new roof added to the old base is evident in this view.

Scotland

Above: Some 10 hours later on the 15 August 1976 and 24107 is seen stabled on Haymarket depot. Behind it are 27109, 47273, 26003 and 27202. Also present that evening were 08763, 25012, 25028, 25237, 27112, 27208, 47402 and 47517.

Above: This view was captured from an Edinburgh to Glasgow push-pull train that was hauled by a pair of Class 27s on 8 July 1978. With 55003 "Meld" dominating the scene, we also see 27019 and an unidentified Class 47 in the background.

TRACTION MAINTENANCE DEPOTS

Above: These next few images were taken on Sunday 9 July 1978, when in addition to the 39 locomotives listed in Table 8, there were a total of 16 DMU vehicles resting from their duties on the suburban routes from Edinburgh.

Below: After it had arrived on a passenger service from Inverness, 26036 has buffered up to 25023 at Haymarket on 9 July 1978. To their right is the two-track refuelling building and to its right the edge of the three-track heavy maintenance shed is just visible.

Scotland

Above: 40123 and 08711 are seen inside the main maintenance shed at Haymarket on 9 July 1978.

Above: A typical range of motive power is seen both outside and inside the main maintenance shed at Haymarket on 9 July 1978. From left to right are 46031, 40062, 47467, 55022 and 25087.

Above: This final view of Haymarket on 9 July 1978 sees 27110 in the wheel lifting bay alongside another unidentified Class 27 and to their right 47516 catches the sun while it is stabled outside.

Scotland

Below left & below: On 3 September 1979, a group of us headed from Cardiff to the Isle of Lewis for a holiday and we broke our drive in Edinburgh, where we stayed at the Youth Hostel near Haymarket depot. Just after 19.00 that evening 40160 can be seen with 20205 and 25046, and Edinburgh Castle is visible in the background. There were a total of 25 DMU vehicles and 29 locomotives present, including 55006 "THE FIFE AND FORFAR YEOMANRY" which is shown resting inside the shed.

TRACTION MAINTENANCE DEPOTS

Above: 08564 is seen outside the refuelling and inspection shed at Millerhill on 10 July 1978. Note the "64B" painted on its buffer beam, which is the pre-TOPS depot code for its home depot Haymarket. This is most likely an informal marking applied by Haymarket's staff, as the 64B depot code had been superseded by the TOPS code "HA" five years earlier.

Below: The Cambridge University Railway Club organised an official brake van ride from Millerhill on 25 March 1981. Members could join the crew of 8J25, the morning trip freight that ran to Bathgate and back behind 26025. This arrived back at Millerhill Yard at around 13.00, when we passed this line up which consisted of 40152 (nearest), 45004, 46036 and 37169. The former Waverley Route main line is on the right, as the first section of this as far as Bilston Glen Colliery had been retained and the truncated Up Sorting Sidings are behind the locomotives.

Scotland

Above: 26003 stands inside the single track shed at Millerhill on the evening of 24 April 1986, after having spent the day hauling rakes of loaded MGR wagons to Cockenzie Power Station.

Below: Also on 24 April 1986, 26004 is seen stabled alongside 37096 and 20223. Behind the Class 26 the former Up Hump Control Tower looms large. The hump itself had closed in 1970 as a consequence of the closure of the Waverley Route to Carlisle.

TRACTION MAINTENANCE DEPOTS

Above: 20208 stands on the fuel oil track at Millerhill on 24 April 1986. The four TTA tank wagons will be returned to Grangemouth once their contents have been dispensed.

EASTFIELD

It was always worth the trek to Eastfield because it was one of the few depots where more than 50 locomotives would be stabled each weekend. By far the best way to the depot was via Springburn station, as it was a ten-minute walk from there. Interestingly, the Locoshed Directory suggested a much longer route involving a 45-minute walk from Glasgow Queen Street station. The depot was rebuilt for diesels on the site of the old steam shed and opened in 1971. For much of its life it had an allocation of over 200 locomotives, making it the largest depot in Scotland. It had a fairly short life as a diesel locomotive depot, closing in 1992 and it was demolished shortly thereafter. Scotrail then repurposed the site and built a new depot for servicing DMUs; this opened in 2004 and is still active.

Class	Locos on 17 August 1974	Locos on 8 July 1978
06	06003 & 06004	06003
08	08227, 08323, 08348, 08721, 08731, 08733, 08754, 08851 & 08852	08147, 08227, 08348, 08402, 08442, 08561, 08693, 08753, 08764 & 08851
20	20010, 20024, 20034, 20089, 20095, 20096, 20111, 20112, 20137 & 20138	20085, 20091, 20096, 20100, 20102, 20109, 20124, 20138, 20146 & 20206
24–25	24004, 24005, 24011, 24097, 24099, 24107, 24117, 25228 & 25229	24006, 25006, 25007, 25023, 25079, 25109, 25227, 25228 & 25247
26	26037 & 26039	None
27	27003, 27009, 27010, 27015, 27021, 27023, 27032, 27039, 27041, 27043, 27044, 27104, 27105, 27109, 27111 & 27206	27003, 27007, 27011, 27014, 27016, 27018, 27025, 27032, 27033, 27038, 27043, 27102, 27111, 27112, 27201, 27206 & 27209
37	37133, 37144 & 37150	37108, 37111, 37145 & 37157
47	47211 & 47466	47015, 47208, 47297, 47424 & 47466

Table 10: The locos that were present at Eastfield on two dates during the 1970s. In addition, nine DMU vehicles were present on 8 July 1978.

Right: 06003, which seems to have gained a superfluous digit before its number, is stabled at the buffer stops on one of the outside sidings at Eastfield on 8 July 1978. Also visible on the siding are 08227, 27016 and 08348.

Scotland

Above: On 17 August 1976, during the long hot summer, 26040 and 26014 are seen on one of the refuelling roads at Eastfield depot.

Above & right: These two views were taken on 8 July 1978; one after climbing a lighting mast and another looking from a different direction at ground level. They show something of the number of engines that could be seen at Eastfield. Some of those that are most prominent in the aerial view are 27014, 08402, 20085 and 20146. At ground level, from left to right are an unidentified Class 08, 25007, 08402, 37157, 25079, 20085 and 47466. Details of what else was seen on the depot that day are summarised in Table 10.

Scotland

TRACTION MAINTENANCE DEPOTS

Above & below: These further two images from 8 July 1978 show 27033 in the heavy maintenance section at Eastfield, with 27034 just visible behind. Outside this building, we see 20146, 20134 & 20109 and an unidentified Class 08.

Scotland

GLASGOW WORKS

Glasgow Works was a ten-minute walk from Barnhill station and I only ever visited it once during the summer of 1976. Table 11 lists the locomotives that were present that day. The Works finally closed in 2019 and it was initially rumoured that the site was to be acquired by the main line charter operator Locomotive Services for use as a Scottish base, but this does not appear to be going ahead.

Table 11: The locos that were present within Glasgow Works on 17 August 1976. 20014 and 27006 both carried two numbers at the time. As well as their recently-applied TOPS numbers, 20014 and 27006 both still wore their respective former numbers, 8014 and 5352. In addition to these locomotives, there were a variety of electric multiple unit vehicles, coaches and wagons scattered across the site.

Class	Locos
06	06003
08	08561, 08720, 08852 & 08882
20	20014, 20002, 20012, 20019, 20038, 20074, 20096, 20104, 20149 & 20201
24	24002, 24004 & 24011
25	25003, 25022, 25024, 25068 & 25091
26	26004, 26008, 26016, 26036, 26042 & 26043
27	27003, 27006, 27020, 27028, 27029, 27030, 27037, 27039 & 27040

Left & below: When I visited Glasgow Works on 17 August 1976, several withdrawn locomotives were present, some of which were in a partially dismantled state. The demolition of 20074, which had only entered service 15 years earlier, was evidently underway. Nearby, 24002 & 24004, which had both been withdrawn in 1975, wouldn't last much longer as the pair would be scrapped here in 1977.

TRACTION MAINTENANCE DEPOTS

Above & below: On 17 August 1976 Glasgow suburban EMU 303071 undergoes major repairs in the main workshop at Glasgow Works. 26016 was another of the locomotives being dismantled, with 20074 visible behind it.

Scotland

POLMADIE

The depot was a 45-minute walk from Glasgow Central but my recollection is that we always caught a bus from St. Enoch square when visiting Polmadie in the 1970s. The site began maintaining diesels in 1963, when the old two-road steam workshops were repurposed. Diesels were also stabled in large numbers in the adjacent six-track steam depot which underwent very little alteration. By the mid-1970s the site was in a poor state and by 1978 stabling of locomotives had been moved to the south side of the West Coast Main Line (WCML) while the main depot area was redeveloped. Polmadie thrives today and sidings on both sides of the WCML remain in use to service the Pendolinos used on the WCML, the diesel & electrical multiple units that form suburban services and Caledonian Sleeper trains.

Class	Locos on 17 August 1974	Locos on 8 July 1978
08	3089, 3388, 3396, 3541, 08447, 08693 & 08719	08173, 08421, 08719, 08721, 08733 & 08853
17	8504, 8542, 8546, 8548, 8550, 8551, 8557, 8563, 8573, 8607, 8608, 8612, 8613 & 8616	None
20	20015, 20078, 20079, 20080, 20083, 20093, 20099, 20105, 20108, 20116, 20117 & 20223	20020, 20027, 20049, 20086, 20093, 20095, 20105, 20107, 20108, 20117, 20119, 20126 & 20191
24–25	24098	25013, 25068, 25246, 25287 & 25288
26–27	26014, 26040, 27028, 27030, 27113 & 27123	26026, 27020 & 27034
37	37145, 37173 & 37204	37150 & 37155
40	40089 & 40167	40014
47	47281, 47357 & 47471	47211 & 47240
50	50040	None
81–87	None	84010 & 87030

Table 12: The locos that were present at Polmadie Depot on two dates during the mid-1970s. Of the locos seen on the July 1978 date, these were within the works building on the eastern side of the West Coast Main Line: 08173, 20027, 20086, 20119, 20191, 25013, 25068, 37150, 47211 & 47470.

Below: On 8 July 1978, the three engines found at the end of these three rows of stabled traction at Polmadie were 08853, 20020 and 20107. The full list of locomotives that were present that day, which included representatives from nine different classes, is summarised above in Table 12.

TRACTION MAINTENANCE DEPOTS

Scotland

Opposite & this page: Some of my earliest successful Scottish depot pictures were taken on 17 August 1974 using my father's aged and battered Agfa Silette, and the film was then processed in my wardrobe! They included these four taken at Polmadie depot on Saturday 17 August 1974, during a day trip from my grandparents' house near Blackburn. Firstly 40089 is seen outside The Works, so named because the two-road diesel maintenance shed had been converted from Polmadie's steam locomotive repair shops. A total of 14 withdrawn Clayton Class 17s were present that day, some of which were photographed for posterity, including 8504 which can be seen in the second image. The third view shows some of the locomotives lined up outside the old six-road steam shed; from left to right are 37145 complete with a makeshift headcode, 20099 and 20093. The elderly gentleman wearing a trilby hat was the shed foreman who made sure we got our pictures and that we then left the premises safely! Finally 47357 in two-tone green livery is also seen outside the steam shed. A total of 48 locomotives were noted that day and these are summarised in Table 12.

TRACTION MAINTENANCE DEPOTS

Above & below: Nearly four years later, on 8 July 1978, the first photograph shows 47211 and 25068 inside the works at Polmadie, with the external doors behind them. Turning 180 degrees and looking in the other direction sees 20027, behind which is 37150, and then 20119 & 20191 behind 47211. The other locomotives that were present in the depot that day are listed in Table 12.

Scotland

Above & below: Moving to the outside of Polmadie's old works building on 8 July 1978 finds 25013 and some of the many buffers and cabs that were parked up as seen from this interesting angle.

TRACTION MAINTENANCE DEPOTS

HAMILTON

Hamilton was almost exclusively used to store and service the DMUs that worked the Glasgow suburban routes. Consequently, it was rare for diesel locomotives to be onsite during the week, although a couple of Motherwell-allocated engines could sometimes be found there at weekends. The DMU depot closed and was demolished more than 25 years ago, but part of the site is still used by the wagon repair firm EG Steele.

Scotland

Below: On 14 August 1976, this selection of diesel multiple units was found lined up at the buffer stops inside Hamilton depot. The far three units are Class 107s, the one with a headcode panel is a Cravens Class 105 and the train nearest the camera is a Class 116 suburban unit.

MOTHERWELL

The depot at Motherwell was only a 10-minute walk from the station and was always welcoming when I visited throughout the 20-year period covered by this book. Steam finished at the depot in 1967 and two roads inside the former steam workshops were converted to a single-road shed for use by diesels, whilst the rest of the depot was used for light locomotive repairs and wagon repairs. Through the 1970s and 1980s Motherwell was important as a servicing point for freight locomotives and following the closure of Eastfield in 1992, it effectively became the most important diesel depot in Scotland. A major stabling point for the depot was the Up Yard at Mossend, just two miles to the north and in 2009 when the depot at Motherwell closed, DB Schenker (now DB Cargo) opened a single-road servicing shed in the Down Yard at Mossend. The facilities at Motherwell were not demolished and are now being leased to the freight operator Direct Rail Services, keeping the site alive today. Two typical "hauls" of what could be seen at the depot during the 1970s are shown in Table 13.

Class	Locos on 14 August 1976	Locos on 8 July 1978
08	08278, 08279, 08312 & 08313	08313, 08314, 08321, 08437, 08723 & 08735
20	20034, 20055, 20085, 20106, 20120 & 20121	20003, 20007, 20080, 20106, 20110, 20120, 20121 & 20202
25	25004, 25011, 25034, 25087, 25093, 25094, 25229, 25231 & 25244	25034, 25064, 25072, 25083, 25090, 25108, 25209, 25230 & 25244
26	None	26034
37	37147	None
40	40112 & 40145	None
47	47053, 47351, 47472 & 47550	47197

Table 13: The locos that were present at Motherwell on two dates during the 1970s.

Above, above right & right: These three images were taken at Motherwell depot on 8 July 1978. Firstly 20080 and 20003 rest at the front of two lines of Class 20s which are stabled round the back of the shed. The second photograph shows a selection of Class 25s and the old steam shed which is one of the few such facilities in the country that remains in use today. Finally 26034 is seen at rest; the other locomotives that were present that particular Sunday are listed in Table 13.

Scotland

TRACTION MAINTENANCE DEPOTS

Below, bottom & right: Three images from 4 July 1989 which show that by then the roof of the old steam shed had been replaced at the south-west end of the building (when compared to the previous images taken in 1978). Outside the two diesel servicing roads of the shed, which are at the south end of the building, is 26014. Inside the two-track shed are 37320, 37201 and an unidentified Class 26. Finally a row of four shunters which includes 08738, 08588 and 08732, is seen from the depot's refuelling track.

Scotland

Above: On 20 June 1990, 60005 is undergoing crew training at Motherwell. It is being refuelled after a test run, when it hauled 29 HEA coal hoppers to Millerhill and back via Shotts. The Class 60s were to become the standard motive power for the bulk of the traffic to and from Ravenscraig Steelworks and the Ayrshire Coalfield.

Above right & right: On 25 June 1991, 26040 is stabled outside, at the north-east end of Motherwell's two-track light maintenance building. I was fortunate to ride in its cab that afternoon as it handled the last ever trip from Mossend to Dalmuir Riverside. The trip ran without traffic, which I suspect was for my benefit! Inside the heavy maintenance part of the complex on the same day was the new order, in the form of 60022. The addition of working platforms necessitated having just one track inside what had previously been a two-track workshop.

Stop
Await instructions
26 040

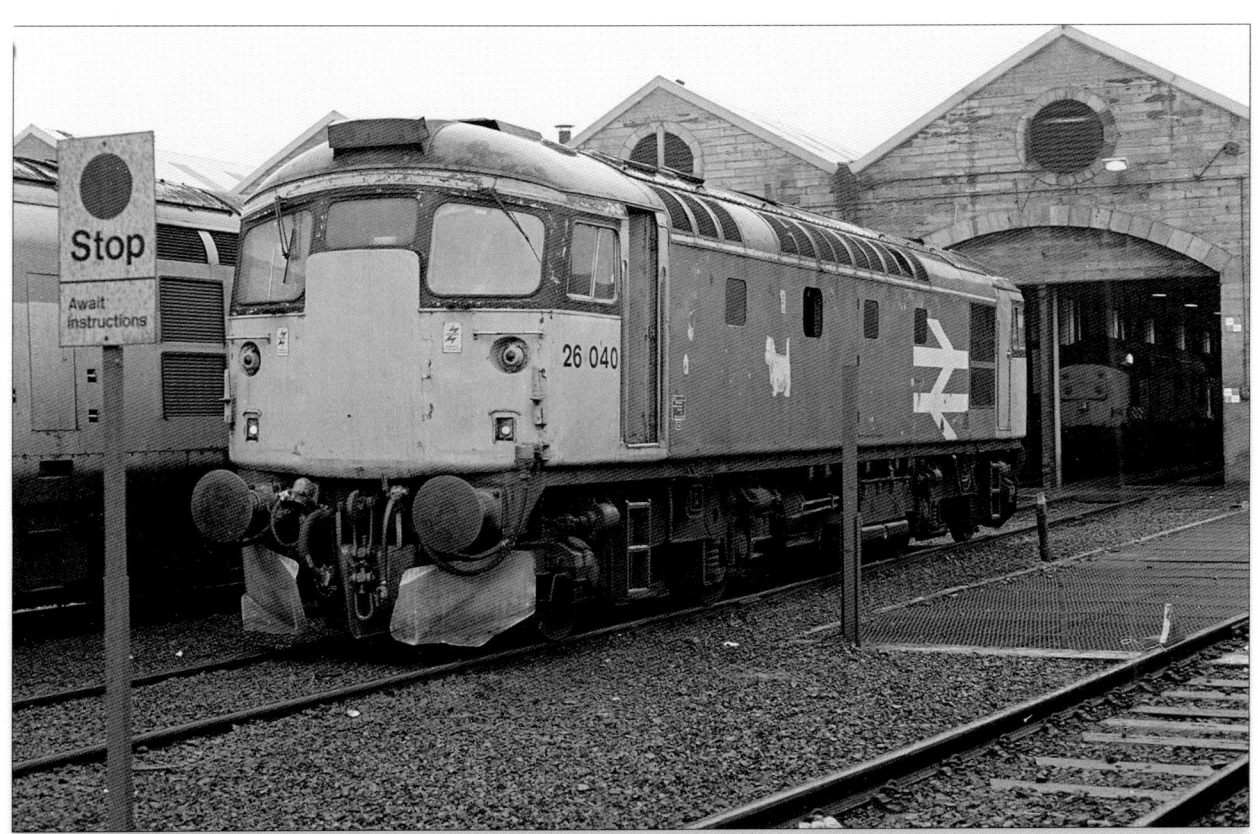

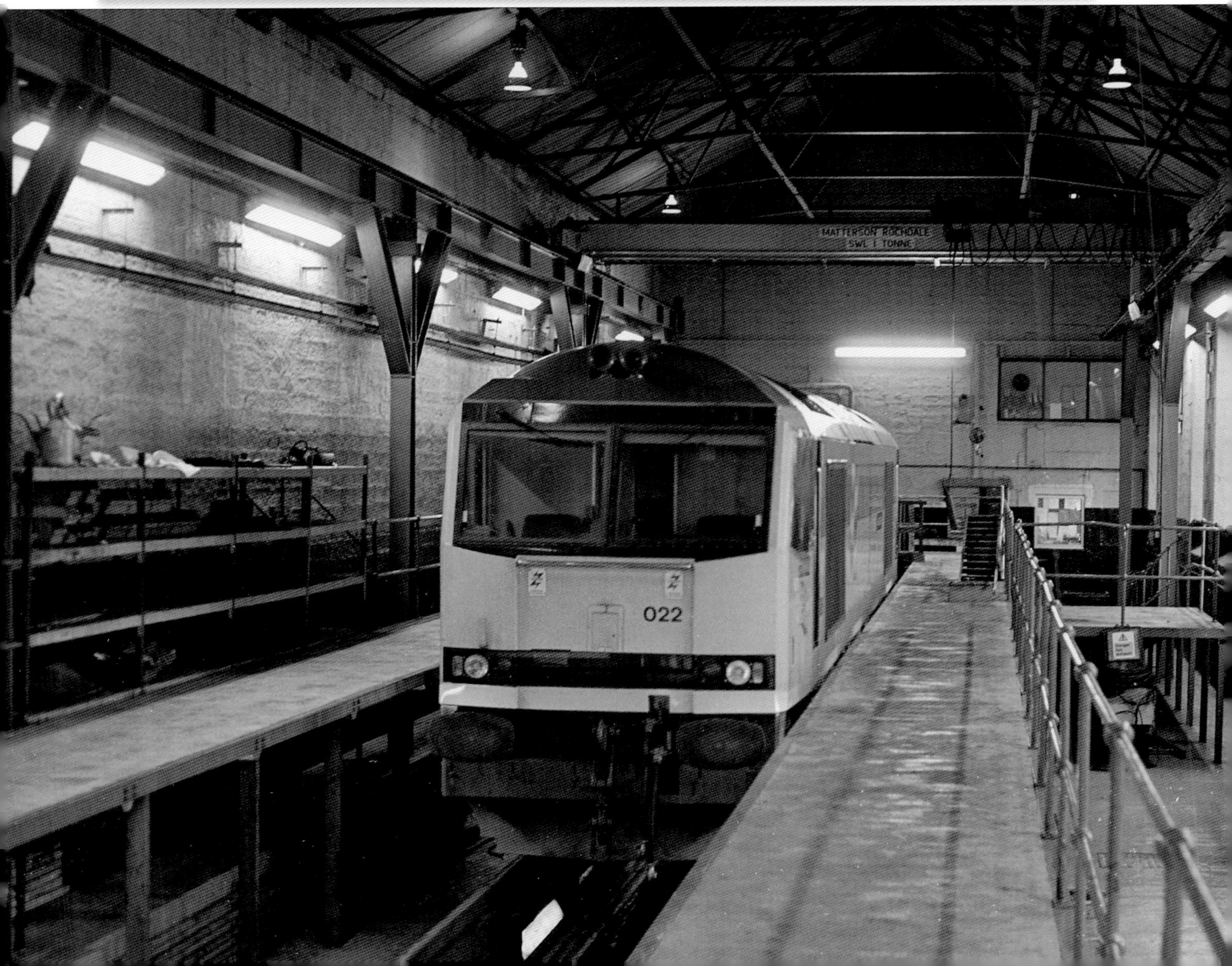
MATTERSON ROCHDALE
SWL 1 TONNE
022

TRACTION MAINTENANCE DEPOTS

Above: Throughout the 1980s and 1990s locomotives were stabled at the south end of the Up Sorting Sidings at Mossend. This typical line-up was found on 25 June 1991, which from left to right consists of 08938, 37128, 90044, 90040, 90029 and 26040 as it waits to take me to Dalmuir Riverside.

Scotland

Above: A trio of what would now be considered "vintage" electric locomotives stand in the stabling tracks at the south end of Mossend Yard on 11 September 1985. From left to right are 86232, 81012 and 85024. Each of these will be deployed on evening departures to the south; the 86 will take over an Inverness to Euston express and the other two will haul evening Speedlink freights to England.

Left: The south end of the Up Yard at Mossend was often used to stable up to a dozen locomotives, although on 25 June 1991, 90050, 90041 & 90040 were all that was to be found there. The AC electric trio carry Railfreight Distribution livery, which would soon become extinct with the end of Speedlink. 90050 & 90041 have been attached to the consist of 6V93, the Speedlink departure to Stoke Gifford. This working previously ran to Severn Tunnel Junction, having done so for two decades until the yard there closed in 1987.

TRACTION MAINTENANCE DEPOTS

AYR

The depot was only a 10-minute walk from Newton-on-Ayr station and generally held between 5 and 10 locomotives on weekdays and around 15 to 20 at weekends. What I found during my August 1976 visit is summarised in Table 14. As with many Scottish depots, my experience was that it was relatively easy to wander round. Having opened as a diesel facility in 1966, the depot closed 41 years later in 2007. The closure was a consequence of the gradual collapse of Scottish coal production, most of which came from the Ayrshire Coalfield. The main diesel shed was eventually demolished in 2019. Minor stabling points for locomotives allocated to Ayr during the 1970s were Ardrossan Harbour and Dumfries. Ardrossan was allocated four shunting locomotives to handle the traffic at the nearby chemical plants and within the harbour.

Class	Locos
08	08144, 08344, 08430, 08449 & 08730
20	20015, 20027, 20108, 20114, 20115, 20116, 20117, 20124, 20137 & 20202
25	25001, 25002, 25009, 25084 & 25239

Table 14: The locos that were present at Ayr depot on 16 August 1976.

Below & right: On 16 August 1976, 25239 heads a row of Class 20s that starts with 20027. The engines are parked for the weekend as no coal trains ran on Saturdays or Sundays during the 1970s. Nearby, 25009 is being refuelled and the indifference of the shed staff to a 16 year old photographer was typical of many similar sites in Scotland where the staff just let visiting enthusiasts wander round.

TRACTION MAINTENANCE DEPOTS

Above, above right & right: My final visit to Ayr depot before it closed was on 24 March 1999. Although this is a little outside the timeframe of this book, the images illustrate the changes that had taken place over 23 years since my 1976 visit. Present that day was 08441 undergoing minor maintenance, 37217 inside the inspection shed and 66017 & 60014 at the refuelling point.

Scotland

TRACTION MAINTENANCE DEPOTS

Above: Under the cover of the maintenance shed at Ayr depot on the following day, 25 March 1999, was 60053 "Nordic Terminal". By this time, the Ayrshire Coalfield had contracted considerably and only four or five locomotives were needed each day to service the Chalmerston branch and Killoch Washery, from where coal was dispatched to Drax Power Station and the coal disposal points at New Cumnock. The massive reserves in the area were never fully exploited as many of the country's coal-fired power stations were being closed. In addition to those illustrated on the previous two pages, the other locomotives present on the depot that day were 56004 and 60053, while 60025 and 60032 were working locally on coal trains.

Above: Four Class 08s were stabled at Ardrossan Harbour on 17 August 1976; the two shown on this photograph are 08345 & 08446 and 08343 & 08476 are out of sight. At the time Ardrossan was a major port for the ferries to both the Isle of Arran and the Isle of Man. Until the 1970s it also handled a fair amount of wagonload freight and the shunters stabled there were employed on trip workings to the ICI plant at Stevenston and to the British Steel Corporation's Glengarnock Works.